WITHDRAWN

Feb 2013

THE ORACLE OF
HOLLYWOOD BOULEVARD

THE ORACLE OF
HOLLYWOOD BOULEVARD

Dana Goodyear

W. W. NORTON & COMPANY

NEW YORK · LONDON

For information about permission to reproduce selections from this book,
write to Permissions, W. W. Norton & Company, Inc., 500 Fifth Avenue,
New York, NY 10110

For information about special discounts for bulk purchases, please contact
W. W. Norton Special Sales at specialsales@wwnorton.com or 800-233-4830

Manufacturing by The Maple Press
Production manager: Devon Zahn

Library of Congress Cataloging-in-Publication Data

Goodyear, Dana.
The oracle of Hollywood Boulevard / Dana Goodyear. — 1st ed.
p. cm.
Includes bibliographical references.
Poems.
ISBN 978-0-393-08246-3
I. Title.
PS3607.O5923O73 2013
811'.6—dc23
                                    2012034410

W. W. Norton & Company, Inc.
500 Fifth Avenue, New York, N.Y. 10110
www.wwnorton.com

W. W. Norton & Company Ltd.
Castle House, 75/76 Wells Street, London W1T 3QT

1 2 3 4 5 6 7 8 9 0

FOR BILLY

CONTENTS

I.

A C K N O W L E D G M E N T S

The author wishes to thank the editors of the following publications, in which these poems, sometimes in different form or with different titles, first appeared.

The New Yorker: "Next," "The Bowerbirds," "Dog Whistle," and "Dormant"
The Atlantic: *"Objet petit a"*
The Yale Review: "Kit for Civilization"
The Colorado Review: "Springtime in Hollywood," "Abundance," "Separate People," and "Spider Season"
Canteen: "Fig," "Quickening," and "An Old Misogynist"
The Daily Beast: "Natural Disaster"
Slake: "Freeway"
The Rattling Wall: "The Singing Bowl" and *"Lüsterweibchen"*

THE ORACLE OF
HOLLYWOOD BOULEVARD

I.

SPRINGTIME IN HOLLYWOOD

I returned: to the bleached light
and the birdlife,
miniature, coked, afraid to stop.
To the drowsy jacarandas
getting naked in the street,
and the filaments of carnelian
in the sidewalk cracks.
Capillaries bursting
in the leaf's pink cheek.
An engine idling behind
a closed white door.

NEXT

The message of even those raised from seed,
their small hands blastomeres, overloved
for what they are, over-looked-at. *Watch me go.*
We were digging the bed when a woman
appeared at the gate, her face torqued red,
crying openmouthed and silently. Do you know
Angela, she said. Angela is dead.
Later, we heard about her gold teeth out,
a cup of golden liquid underneath her cot.

I learned: nasturtium comes from "twisted nose."
Then found two deep ruts
around the roots, the strangled faces
touched but silent, saying someone has been here.

WEDDING MONTH

Moving forest, nurserymen stagehands: April.
Grafting life on mineral patches, masking
naked, dry ground, Mexican radio on.
       Carpenters at noon.

We find grave goods, excavating backyard trenches.
Tarnished marble, maculate, like a bad eye.
Dog bones, dogs' bones. Delicate skull in Hefty
       burial plastic.

Arson, drifter, cigarette. Griffith Park a
-live with flickers. Mystery water floods the
pulsing green and argentine yard. Coyotes.
       Married in four days.

ABUNDANCE

The fruited tree
with her orange cheeks
ballooned, puffed gills, in treacly
wind, or, if you like,
the spill of the tanked gold sun.
Do you still love me? Now what
kind of a question is that.
And yet it can't be taken back.
The bachelor-lady's house wants
filling, the drip line's laid below
our promising new life.

SEPARATE PEOPLE

I have been beside you
all night like soaped windows,
like the iron fence
around a city park, like the hedge
whose gray-green musk and webs
remind you of Greenwich,
solitary morning prayer,
the country-club policy on Jews.
"That's why I'm a mountain,
I am cold and pointy at the top,"
I said, asleep,
the Oracle of Hollywood Boulevard.
Your sad question:
Where were we?
Then, knowing that you weren't,
Was I there?

THE BOWERBIRDS

As if we were leaving
the small forest tower that you built,
with a moss carpet and mosquito chandeliers,
and laughing at it.
But we would never break this way,
loose, affectionate, wry.
You straighten,
add an ornament.
This is somehow part of our staying.
If you left, a black cape would flap
like a crow winging,
and I would make a hundred harried calls.

DOG WHISTLE

Up the road, a glittering army
marshals at the line; light turns,
and the blood between us tightens like a rope,
the anchor digs its heel.
Love is a jumper, going over like the water of a dam.

Killing off the lazy ones,
sending hot air rushing through the grates,
the city gets prepared. We have tape, a radio.
The newspaper keeps chaos just at bay.
Old people, full of feeling, inch away.

Want hearts. Make a religion of sex.
Separate the sick. Teach the smart ones
greed. Decide small pieces are important,
and divide them (two for you, one for him).
Tell your story on a bowl.
Paint skulls and weapons; give them eyes
and smiles. Learn to deal.
Soften, grow more pompous. Exult
in the love between this and that,
or you and your god. Abstract. Talk peace.
When the enemy comes, eat this.

THE DISAPPEARANCE

A yellow veil dropped down at evening,
and when it lifted everyone was gone.
Good mothers fled their young for parts unknown—
no "fall dwindle" but a stillborn spring.
Hive beetles and wax moths came not near.

Collapse, disorder, all these words were said,
while nursery rhymes and jingles went unsung.
Come witch hour, the old red telephone rang:
You had noticed that if you moved, you bled.
I was your keeper, sleeping through my watch.

Infection wraps itself around your bones
whispering all kinds of bad advice
about the fragile strangeness of a life.
Your body now a hive whose bees have flown.
Husband! Call them back.

NATURAL DISASTER

The princess in the black pit has bound
hands and a wildflower diadem. Extinct beasts
sucked her bones clean.

The desert creeps at the rate of fingernails;
the abbreviation for street
is the same as that for saint.

In the doctor's waiting room, a young man
screams into a telephone "What the fuck?"
which is exactly what everyone else is wondering.

On the periphery, tents pitched
under overpasses cant
against the dirty wind.

Congratulations, Beauty. You are rich enough
to drive your own limousine
to your own funeral.

Chandelier, swimming pool, EKG
all sashay together on the count of three.
Abracadabra, you are free.

WILD FIRE

1. Dormant

We want this.
The end to sleeping, the bittersweet
arousal, the peeling back, the soft bath
in resin, the release. It can't come quick
enough, the hot touch that breaks the crust
and lets us go. Hear it now: a crackling,
as the woods begin to sing alongside the birds.
To cry out. To be transformed, like Daphne
back into a girl. Pine—as if our very nature
demanded that we long without relief. But the cone
is like a shotgun on the wall; it must erupt.
All it takes is one dumb fuck, trigger-happy,
with a six-pack and bad aim,
to fill the world with flames.

2. The Witch Creek

Innocent at first. Milk-breath
in the oaks like the warm pant
between a morning lake face and the sky.
I have my own self-heating heart, I fly—
send an ember through the trapdoor
in the roof, skinny up the creosote, blacken
the windows. Think of an appetite growing
indiscriminate—heroes will do, or swine.
Curse me, and my taste
for licked wire. The crows are mine,
flapping like the torn black sheets of ash
that waft over empty neighborhoods.
Come away, come away, as the old drama says.
Smell my meat and feathers.

3. Sundowner

From above, scorch marks
shadow missing trees, ample as ink
shot by a panicked octopus;
brain-black prints of sex secrets;
Escher's optical illusions;
or a gypsy deck (couple &
skull, maiden & crone).
Heat rushes down the bristling
canyon necks, funneling the tumbleweeds
and horses to the sea. Late
afternoon confusion settles in
(Where am I and who are you?)
as each breath brings more particulate
and the incense of a beached whale blows amber in the air.

FREEWAY

Alongside this, a river: somewhere head-
waters, somewhere a mouth.
It begins with thought and ends with speech,

while the road just drains and drains, gray
nervous miles. I drive all day under a strike surface
scratched by skywriters' mistakes, through the city

bleeding silver like a video game,
past Nadaland, past Mojave, toward the bodies
decomposing in the quiet valleys

killers used to ranch. Behind me,
in my mind, the lurid birds of paradise
bend their orange faces toward the pool

to drink, but the pool is full
of flames, and the trees are ash shadows,
and the sky's so dark night-blooming whites

release themselves to moths
too singed to reach them. The yellow vine
presses its wax ear against the warping glass,

and the deck chairs, pale and worked
as skeletons, somehow hold their ground.

II.

DAYLIGHT SAVINGS

There was a time when the world outside
fascinated: shagged palm legs like the
drumsticks of a green rooster; spiral
chimney of neighbor's guest cottage;
gray dove on the wire. It might have been
the sparrow Catullus envied
I looked at it so much, while you
lay facedown in the sheets.
Today, the clear grease shadow of that dove
was ghosted on the windowpane,
and I stayed with you inside the room,
as the warm white walls became a womb.

CONCEPTION

This time of year the snakes leave their old skins
hanging in the Meyer lemon tree—
afterbirth, carcass, or nude hose.

"Choose Life" says the hand-drawn sign
at the edge of the almond-pale, crystal-pink grove
on Interstate 5.

A poll of teenagers in Hollywood asks
"What is the opposite of youth?"
Overwhelmingly, they answer "death."

Meanwhile, in the Magic Garden, the grass
begins to build a crusty yellow tip, ice forms
on the volcano's lip, the cone hole yawns clean.

Inject clear liquid where I mark the X.
We are late—e.g., these bruised white
blossoms on the ground.

My eyes are turning dull.
Soon I'll bite my handler,
and glide out into morning, beaded, self-made, glistening.

FIG

Miniature woman, all womb.
I don't see you, brown,
uncamouflaged as the bottom
or nipple in a dream,
till the beetle's buried
himself to the neck
in your soft flesh.

OBJET PETIT A

Remember its pulse
on the salt-swollen porch,
both body and gash,

that starfish
you rescued, stranded
when found

on the winter beach,
a hand pantomiming
klepto-

mania: Stop, thief.
Slick, warm, red clot,
who knew what it meant

by living. It should have turned
hard, into ornament,
but stayed wet, like guilt.

SPIDER SEASON

A fingerprint on air
holding, paradoxically, a small
eight-fingered leather hand.
After a certain point,
I thought of it as a woman not a man,
a purse with a slew of bodies
and its own death inside.

FISHING

Suddenly, everyone's a naturalist
and a mystic and a killer, tenderly brutal.

They seem to be such individualists, jumping
in the sun, practical as iron needles
darning their wet shroud.

The child catches one of keeping weight.
We call her pregnant, the female full of eggs—
but she is pregnant the way a newborn girl is,
with everything she'll ever have.

Twilight, we eat her raw,
and then we eat her roe.

THE SINGING BOWL

1. Hysteric

In the eaves of the glass house
on the cliff a globe light goes on.

Miles down, I'm the girl in the rushes
at the beginning of the film
or the animal whose vertebra
found in a dry creek bed
someone will make a whistle of.

2. Make-Believe

Beside the white garage,
where the dog was chained
and the lady manikin lived alone,
weaving God's-eye spiderwebs
between her slender forefinger and thumb,
my sister, thinking of a recent sex lesson
and how it was said I'd popped
out like a watermelon seed,
spooned some dirt into her mouth
and a slimy black teardrop
the color of the tar that blistered
on the gravel drive, and waited.

3. Old Wives' Tale

Want, don't want,
don't drink, get drunk,
never, anymore, think,
wake in the night and insist.

"The last flower is the best,"
some fool told you in your despair.
Now you carry the phrase
in your wallet like a tranquilizer pill.

What I know: Let's make
a baby is only a joke
if the man says it.
And the bowl only sings empty.

The idea of a child, like a bonsai:
a small close work
representing acres of time.
The distant figure standing before you,

viewed through the binoculars' back end,
is made from things that want to fly
apart so violently the doctor
calls them "blasts."

4. Quickening

The cracked blue egg
on the step and cast
of cold-sweat shadow
underneath the sycamores
when I nearly missed
the oncoming car:
this marked the beginning
of what I thought
was motherhood.

5. News

Unloosed, the silver helium balloon flies over fields,
while the child crouches in the attic hoping never to be found.

My mind-cry becomes an infant's,
calling "Stay." It sounds like bleating.

If only you would drink my blood and let me breathe for you.
But you are wild, and startle at the salt lick.

6. The Dreams of Pregnant Women

"Water, talking animals, tall buildings, sex . . ."
witnessed crimes, spilled fluids, falling down
an elevator shaft, seducing the interrogator,
his one fat finger pressed against my lips.

There I was, on my knees, wailing,
while my mother searched the bedding
for the baby and found stained lace
dresses and discarded china dolls instead.

Her recurring dream, she told me
later on the phone, was that she had a baby
she forgot to feed. Then, after a pause,
"I guess I'm the baby."

7. Fairy Tale

Thumbelina did not want Toad or Mole,
but loved a sparrow she thought dead (sick girl).
Later, she married a prince who lived inside a flower.

Sex in Your Garden, by Angela Overy, says that in every flower
lives a woman *and* a man. The pollen enters the "stigma,"
from the Greek "to prick." The danger is selfing.

Forgotten in an upstairs room, we came upon a scene
of theatrical decay, the once-white lilies suffering,
petals turned the sulfur-purple of dead skin fallen to the floor.

I thought of myself, shot through with testosterone—
magnificent, disoriented, bleeding
from the ears. Stranded, while the surf advanced.

8. Loving the Invisible

My sister knew a boy whose mother left;
just "moth" was tattooed to his chest:
a cocoon, and the thing that flew from it.

As of today, mine has fingerprints
and skin that light could pass through,
if there were light in there.

9. Ghost Heart

The scientist keeps
a mouse heart in a glass
bulb, a wet white blob,
like cotton soaked in alcohol.

She washes it with soap
to break the old cells down,
and makes a scaffold for new
ones to cleave to. It starts
to twitch; it starts to act
like it's a heart.

In the lab, someone in a white coat
shouts, "Doris, it's healing."

10. From Life

"What is shocking in art?" my friend asks—not sex,
we agree, not anymore, then stop before a rubbery
gray tail leading from a mound of dust:
a few coarse hairs swept into a pile, a gnarl of foot,
no meat, no bones, no face. No, not even this.

We pass the flowering elderberry bushes, smelling of sperm.
What is shocking, my friend says at last, is to include
your children in your art without their consent.

III.

LÜSTERWEIBCHEN

A chandelier formed from a pair of antlers attached to a wooden carving
of a woman's bust, popular in Germany during the Renaissance.

Polychrome torso,
big rack screwed
into her back,
she dangles from

the ceiling with her
hands full
of dazzling fat
and light,

a mother at a birth-
day party with
a white sheet
cake, only carved,

like the desperate
female souls
that pull themselves
through walls in old

whaling towns,
silently screaming,
Can't you see
this house is on fire?

The antlers make
her a saint
of sex, a siren
rendered by a land-

locked hand, who
dreams of animal
hybrids mounted
on club walls:

the antelabbit, aunt
benny, stagbunny.
In life, probably
a rabbit

infected with
papillomavirus
but in myth
a creature whose

milk is medicine,
who breeds
during electrical
storms, and who

was painted
in dead seriousness
by Joris Hoefnagel,
of Antwerp,

in 1575,
and which I saw
for the first time
when I went to look for you

in the men-only
bar at the
hunting lodge
in Ligonier,

where I almost
choked to death
on iceberg lettuce
at the age of eight,

but for the
Heimlich and
a doctor in the house.
I was hungry.

And where there
were hidden passages,
a tower, and a library
with a revolving

shelf, rooms
in rooms, stocked
with Prohibition-
era booze.

Children shouldn't
see what men
think of, but female
children should.

I went down
to the basement
bowling alley
with its gleaming rows;

the lights hissed
and dimmed and an
older boy said
a prisoner had fried.

In flight those
bones are wings;
on land, ears.
Run, run, run.

Lüster: chandelier;
weibchen: dumb
female, little
woman, hen, bitch, doe.

PORNOGRAPHER AT 84

It's night, according to the peacocks
screaming in the cedar tree. Lights out,
ladies, no more Uno. No more Go Fish.
Today the gardeners sprayed hormones
on the olive tree. In the zoo nursery,
the babies throw themselves against the wire cage.

Year after year, it goes like this. Figs drop
like weights beneath the broad green scales.
Red grenades explode at my touch, deflated
beach balls eddy in the brackish caves.
The girls, they leave and leave but never age.

All I ever tried to do was keep
something of this earth from spoiling.

My smoking jacket grows a pelt of dust.
It is a bathrobe. I shuffle through
the basement quietly. When the fist-sized
birds of daybreak sing, I throw them seeds.

AN OLD MISOGYNIST

I could have argued with him.

Instead, I watched a bulldog—dirty muzzle,
furious yellow-green eye—
mouth the grass,
each mute, oblivious lunge
saying, *Mine, mine,*
until a disembodied hand
pulled it back in line.

MEAT EATER

Tough in the mind and soft in the gut,
eyes of a prison guard who is also prisoner,
the mother pig gestates for three months,
three weeks, and three days, and when she's done
might bite the runt to death, reclaiming her lost calcium.

Inside the slaughterhouse at dawn, I mouthbreathed,
hand on belly (I'm sorry, I'm sorry). The pig,
warm and calm from an electric bath,
took a gloved finger in one dilated eye
as the man in the apron prepared to slit its neck.

AT THE DILDO FACTORY

They are making a mold of a woman.
It will cost $49.99 when done, the boss's son tells me,
a small rubber block with hip bones for handgrips
and a gaping hole—gaping being a term of art. A line of ten
one-night stands: the Mexican, the Goth, the blonde.
This is the alt-chick, someone you could imagine
meeting at a bar. She opens at the knees,
pale, goose-white knees, and, following instructions,
tacks back the layers of her flesh with two fingers,
while a Guatemalan grandmother pours thick pink latex in her lap.
"What are you having?" the dildo son and heir asks me.
The room swells, buoyed on the breath that forms
the word, *Boy*. The best, he says, and raises his fist.
If, later, I have a girl, he reasons, my son will protect her.

In baby CPR, you take a plastic doll and breathe into her shallow
    mouth
to make the chest balloon with air. Two breaths, twenty pumps,
forefinger and index centered between the nipples, which are hard
for ease of demonstration. The dolls are girls, you can tell
by their pink jumpers. They are drowning, they have choked,
they are unconscious, they can't talk, everyone is screaming,
and no one knows how to save them.

SYMPATHETIC MAGIC

I sewed a manikin of my own skin;
now anyone can harm me.
A warning about birds: if they find
your hair they'll build a nest with it.
I keep those wisps beside your picture
in a capsule at my neck, the makings
of a future you.

                          Which is worse—
pain or getting used to it? Somewhere
you are crying, and I parch.

The stranger you reach for at the beach
carries a box that reads "laughter"
on one side. When she moves to touch
your hand I see her word begins with "s."

MIRAGE

I flew through the night to the city. In the morning
it rained. You got in my cab at the corner,
and we went to your empty apartment,

the one with the bed in the living room,
where you used to stop between refugee camps.
On the bed was my quilt; in the bathroom, concealer, a kit.

I remember you here with a bug in your leg, and blood in your eye.
The two of us running, past the cheap chain stores, breathing
exhaust and the sweet burnt scent from the carts,

to the park, toward the women and carriages, the taken-care-of.
Sidestepping the grip of that calm, whatever drug they were on.
But now you are teasing, *The red-eye, like a foreign correspondent*—

meaning that I, too, am single-minded and alone.
We are spies from opposite deserts, meeting
in this third place—opal puddle, glittering spike.

At the airport, I am a suspect, traveling childless
with two days' worth of milk, leaving already,
as you are tonight, for another six weeks. Don't get hurt,

I say to you just this one time, my dear friend. Be careful.

SPARTAN

In peace, boys eat
blood soup and beans,
to keep them hungering
for war. With a cut finger
a woman can paint
her face by accident
when putting on makeup.
She must stay beautiful,
given what a little brute—
petty tyrant (sentimental, cruel)—
it is in her nature to become.
Pity her, she gets to keep nothing.
Her boy cannot remember
what she whispered to him
as they both fell back to sleep.

WONDER

Pale male, milk-fed
veal, softer than
a girl. My child,
I lose my hair like a bargainer
in a fairy tale. After the war,

extra weapons
were melted down
so iron could be added
to our food: a miracle for America,
bone in the bread.

Dear, the body has so many
uses for its materials.
I hear that other mothers
cry, imagining their daughters
giving birth. I cry because someday
you will die and, with you, me.

Your dream: multiple suicides in the infested house.
Mine: full of milk again.

A new made-for-TV science fiction movie has begun.
We drop into the cold lake and hang, breathing.

There is a house, where we watch everything
over-the-shoulder, through a shaky handheld.

Careful! Poison mushroom. False alarm—
that's just the neighbor hacking, not a ghost.

When we emerge, twenty years have passed.
I go searching for our son, the blond one—
how serious his eyes are now.

HOME

Those last days in Hollywood—
Where were we going? We didn't know—
the johns came at midnight
and flung their broken condoms
to the ground; the next day, someone
dumped a car seat at our hedge.
Growling made it worse, those few times
we tried to sleep, curling from the sound
of hunger coming through the bedroom wall.
The furnace burnt the underbrush;
electricity shocked the pool;
dry as hands, the poison leaves
of the poison tree flew from the roof,
where one night, years ago, while
we watched *Play Misty for Me*,
wind played the fence wires'
anguished vocal cords, a lowing
loud as a mourning cow.
This imperfect world.
We are going, we are almost gone.
An accident: your globe dashed,
blue fragments puzzling the floor.
A cosmic question on your face.

NOTES

"The Bowerbirds": Bowerbirds are monogamous birds, in which
   the male of the species woos the female by building an
   elaborate mating den and furnishing it with found objects.
   Sometimes the male will decorate the walls with paint made
   by mixing its saliva with berry juice.

"*Objet petit a*": "The unattainable object of desire," in the
   psychoanalytic theory of Jacques Lacan.

"The Singing Bowl": *Sex in Your Garden*, by Angela Overy, was
   published by Fulcrum Publishing in 1997. "Ghost Heart"
   refers to the work of the cardiac researcher Doris Taylor,
   who uses stem cells to bring back to life the dead hearts of
   laboratory rats.

"*Lüsterweibchen*": William Randolph Hearst had an extensive
   collection of these chandeliers, which he kept at Wyntoon,
   a private estate in Northern California designed by Julia
   Morgan.